Canaries

Everything About
Purchase, Care,
and Nutrition

Thomas Haupt

BARRON'S

Contents

46 Care and Activities

Appendix

The Typical Canary

Canaries, with their chirpy, delightful character, will bring much pleasure to your home. These miniature avian tenors occur in many different color varieties, from lemon yellow to gray-white, and on to pied forms. Because keeping canaries and caring for them is rather uncomplicated compared with larger pet birds, they are among the most popular feathered housemates.

A Brief Canary History

As already suggested by their name, canaries originally came from the Canary Islands, as well as from
the Azores. These birds are closely related to the
European Serin (*Serinus serinus*) and to the European Goldfinch (*Carduelis carduelis*), as well as to
Green finches.

In their native habitat, canaries live primarily in
areas with a dense cover of bushes and trees, as
well as on plantations and in domestic gardens.
An important characteristic of these habitats is
the presence of water holes, where canaries like to
take extensive baths.

From Wild Form to Domesticated Pet

Originally, wild canaries had a plumage that was
greenish brown, which is comparable to that of the
green variety now commonly kept as cage birds.
However, modern canaries are somewhat larger
than the original wild form. When wild canaries
are not breeding (commonly during spring), they
live in loose, small flocks, constantly in search of
food. They feed primarily on the seeds of grasses
and herbs. Occasionally, they will also take the
odd insect or even a fresh dandelion leaf. Canaries
became associated with humans very early in the
period of human habitation, primarily in response
to the availability of food and nesting facilities.
Initially, only wild-caught birds were kept as pets,
purely for the enjoyment of their melodic song,
especially that of males. Captive reproduction was
eventually successful, starting a centuries-long
history of canary breeding. Nowadays, there are
many varieties, which vary substantially in coloration of their plumage and in their singing skills.
It must be noted here that the canary is the only
pet with vocalization skills that have been specifi-
cally altered through dedicated and selective
breeding efforts.

Canaries Conquer the World

When Spain conquered the Canary Islands in 1500, it was also the beginning of the domestication of canaries. It was not long until mutations produced new color varieties. The longer the robust canaries were being bred in captivity, the more diverse the colors and shapes of them became. Initially, there were birds that had yellow spots on the plumage, from which—eventually—pure yellow birds were produced through selective breeding.

Aristocratic Birds

Up to the 19th Century, pure yellow birds were so expensive that only aristocrats or very rich merchants were able to afford these little tenors. Around 1600, Queen Elizabeth I was a particularly enthusiastic canary fan. She even hired staff to take care of her little birds. The first crested canaries were bred in England a mere 50 years later. During the following decades and centuries, canaries were bred and then distributed throughout all of Europe, from Portugal to England and Italy. Monasteries played a particularly important role in this process by selling canaries to boost their income.

Below Ground and Across the Ocean

From the 19th century on, canaries became very popular among working-class people, who bred these birds to increase their income. Underground miners would take canaries down into the mine, where the birds would have a less than pleasant function: When they displayed restless behavior or worse, died, it was a warning to the miners of an oxygen deficiency or the presence of toxic gases in the mine.

At that time, Germany and Tyrol (Austria) were centers of canary-breeding activities. The Hartz Roller Canary, famous for its song, was bred in Germany. Sometimes called the Hartz Mountain Roller, this is the most popular canary variety in captivity. From the middle of the 19th century canaries were exported to the United States;

Smart Beatles hairdo. This picture shows a Gloster variety in white with a crest.

periodically more than 1 million birds were shipped across the Atlantic within a single year.

Three Breeding Lines

Most color varieties of canaries available today originated through selective breeding after 1950. There are now plumage colors that range from white to red and brown, in more than 30 distinct varieties. Within these varieties, it is important to distinguish three main breeding lines: birds selected for (1) their song, (2) their color, and (3) their posture, or "type."

Song canaries These include all canary varieties that are being bred for their song; they are distinguished from one another in song variability and volume. The song of canaries involves certain song "tours," whereby a "tour" consists of interconnected syllables, that is, a strophe. During the 1950s two "tour groups" were established: the "value tours" and the so-called "failure tours." Value tours include, for example, the Knorr, Hollow Roll, Glucke, Whistle, Watertour, Klingel, and Klingelroll. These represent the criteria applied by experts to the singing quality of canaries. The most important representative of song canaries is the Hartz Roller. Other important varieties are the Spanish Timbrado and the Wasserschlaeger canaries, as well as the American Singer.

Color canaries Today there are more than 300 color varieties of canaries. The colors yellow and red come from embedded color pigments (carotenes), picked up through the foods these birds eat. "Color feeding" of certain dietary supplements to maintain the bright shades of yellow or red is common practice among canary keepers. Those birds that are unable to store these carotenes for genetic reasons remain white. The plumage of canaries always con-

Somewhat inconspicuous, more like our finches—this is what a wild canary looks like. Intensive, selective breeding of birds like this has produced more than 300 color varieties.

Canary **Profile**

SCIENTIFIC NAME *Serinus canaria forma domestica.*

WEIGHT This can range from ½ to 1½ ounces (15 to 40 gm).

BODY SIZE The original, wild forms measure about 4¾ inches (12 cm), but specially bred varieties can be up to 8 inches (20 cm) long.

LONGEVITY Normally canaries reach an age of 10 to 12 years; under exceptional circumstances they may live even 15 years or longer.

CLUTCH SIZE The hen lays four to six eggs.

BODY TEMPERATURE Averaging about 107°F (42°C), the body temperature of these little birds is relatively high.

tains one of the basic colors—white, yellow, or red—as well as a specific feather structure: intensive, off-white, or mosaic. "Melanin" birds have—in addition—brown or black markings produced by their own pigments. Their song, however, is generally considered second-rate.

Type canaries: For these varieties, particular emphasis is placed on the way the body is being held, the so-called posture. There are small, smooth-feathered varieties such as the Gloster with a crest, or the English Lizard with a striking pattern of markings. There are also large, smooth-feathered birds, such as the Yorkshire from England or the Bernese (Swiss) canaries. The type varieties are subdivided into smooth-feathered birds and frilled, or curly, birds. Here the typical representatives are Paduan Canaries, an Italian frisé variety, or the Gibber italicus, a type of frisé variety. Crested canaries have a small feather crest, with highly variable coloration.

Lively Housemates

Because of their long period of domestication, canaries are inherently friendly birds. They are easy to care for, which also makes them particularly suitable for novice bird keepers. You should interact with your pet on a daily basis, or possibly keep mul-

"Get out of here, this is my territory!" There can be minor disagreements within a flock of birds. In this picture, the yellow bird is trying to chase the red-mosaic canary away from its perch.

tiple birds. Canaries are not aggressive toward other birds; consequently, canaries can be kept together in a group with finches or quail in an aviary (see page 23). They might also enjoy watching other pets, but keep them safely caged when predatory animals such as dogs, cats, ferrets, or snakes share the house, since these little songsters can easily become prey for larger pets. Canaries do not gnaw on things; in fact, because of the structure of their beaks they are not capable of nibbling on wood or other materials like their sometimes-destructive parrot cousins. In essence, walls and furniture are safe. However, you should be aware that canaries—with a maximum life span of about 15 years—might require care and attention for a relatively long period.

Beguiling Singing

Male canaries use their song principally during courtship, as well as for defining their territory and warning away other males. Canaries have a vast, innate diversity of strophes ("tours") in their song repertoire. The most attractive singing takes place in late summer and in autumn. It is this singing talent that usually entices bird lovers to acquire a canary. The "melodies" are often very impressive and quite pleasing to the human ear—it is nearly always melodic and soft. Consequently, you are not very likely to get complaints from your neighbor.

Each canary variety has its own song, and each male has its particular rendition. If you are purchasing a canary primarily to enjoy its song, you should take your time when selecting your new housemate and visit several breeders so that you can listen to different songs. Males will commence singing as soon as they have reached sexual maturity, so the bird will need to be at least eight to nine months old.

Is a pet canary right for me?

TIPS FROM
CANARY EXPERT
Thomas Haupt

RESPONSIBILITY Canaries can reach an age of up to 10 or 15 years. If the bird belongs to a child, the parents will have co-responsibility for its ongoing health care.

SPACE REQUIREMENTS Always provide your bird with a suitably large cage. If you plan on housing multiple canaries, the cage must be large enough to accommodate all birds without crowding. Allow sufficient space in the cage for the bird to flap its wings freely.

SONG Male canaries like to sing, and their song cannot be simply switched off. Make sure this is something you can tolerate well.

DIRT AND ALLERGIES By dropping small feathers or scattering empty husks of grain around, canaries can be messy. Moreover, feather dander and dried feces can aggravate allergies. If you suffer from allergies, discuss the situation with your doctor before acquiring a bird.

EXPENSES Cage, accessories, food, and the occasional visits to a veterinarian—can you afford to take proper care of your canary?

Canary Portraits

All canaries are yellow? Not by a long shot, although canaries look very attractive in yellow. However, they also come in red, brown, and pied varieties, which are almost equally as popular as yellow birds.

HARTZ ROLLER This is the classic canary as we know it. There are also several different color variations among yellow birds.

GLOSTER Pied birds, here a Gloster with a crest, are a very appealing color variety. The basic color is variable; however, it is always combined with darker patches in the plumage. In the final analysis, visual appeal is a matter of individual taste.

RED CANARIES Red canaries are color mutations that depend on dietary pigments (beta-carotenes) to enhance the red coloration of feathers. However, unless a color supplement is given regularly (by adding carotene or a powder substitute such as canthaxathin) to the drinking water, the bird's deep red color will gradually fade away.

LIZARD A Lizard canary always has a yellow "cap." Such birds are included in the group of type canaries. The bird shown here is a Golden Lizard.

PIED COLOR VARIETY Yellow pied canaries display particularly intense color contrasts. This pied coloration is most attractive when distributed evenly over the entire body.

MELANIN CANARIES These mottled brown birds have less dark (melanin) color pigments, so their brown color tones are lighter and more delicate.

GLOSTER WITHOUT CREST
This particular Gloster without a crest shows considerable melanin embedded throughout the plumage. Therefore, this bird looks almost brownish. The roundish body structure is typical for this variety of type canaries.

RED MOSAIC Depending upon the color intensity, canaries of this color variety are placed into two different types: specimens with an intensive mask, like the bird shown here, belong to Type 2; canaries with less color are included in Type 1.

Canaries as Pets

Immature canaries live in loose flocks or in small groups. Such a way of life provides security against predators, which are more readily seen by many eyes. In addition, it facilitates partner selection and offers the opportunity to establish and maintain social contacts. In captivity, you will be your pet's "flockmate."

Social Birds

If you intend to keep multiple canaries, it's important to understand their social hierarchy. When

canaries are not breeding, they are sociable birds that can readily be kept as a small flock of males and females in an aviary. However, shortly before the onset of the breeding season, males start to define their territory, which they will defend against every other male. At that time, it is prudent to provide a second cage if the first one is not large enough, so that the birds can avoid each other and withdraw. Otherwise, in a small cage those birds at the lower end of the hierarchy will be under permanent stress, because they are constantly driven out of their territories by those birds at the upper end of the social hierarchy. If there are no possibilities for the subordinate birds to withdraw, there can indeed be fatalities. In an appropriately planted and structured large aviary this rarely ever happens. However, in a typical pet cage, it will not be possible to keep more than one breeding pair.

Female canaries among themselves can sometimes be difficult because—just like males—they may become envious of each other's territories. Generally, however, there is social harmony. Usually, keeping just one pair of canaries together works out well. In case you do not want to breed canaries, it is advisable to keep males and females separate from the onset of the mating season (usually starting in March), for about four to five months.

If a male is kept separately, it normally sings a lot to attract a partner. For that reason, in earlier days male canaries used to be kept isolated in small cages in order to stimulate singing. We now

Two Lizard canaries enjoy a play stand.

In general, all small birds are potential prey for cats. Therefore, you should never leave them together unsupervised in the same room.

Canaries can get along well with guinea pigs, hamsters, and similar small animals. Each lives in its own world and pays little attention to the other.

have a better understanding of their need to socialize and explore. Especially if you are not home during the day, provide a large cage with plenty of opportunities to forage, or consider keeping more than one bird. Even a different species of bird in a separate cage can provide companionship when humans aren't around.

Male or Female?

Male as well as female canaries are sociable and usually friendly housemates. If you are particularly interested in a singing canary, you are better off with a male. Determining the sex of canaries, especially that of juvenile birds, is not easy, and is essentially impossible for a nonprofessional. The cloacal opening in mature males is normally slightly cone-shaped, or raised off the body. In females, this anal protrusion is distinctly weaker. Sometimes, you can compare several birds next to each other and see the differences, but this is not always reliable. Song and courtship behavior are reliable indicators in

birds approaching sexual maturity, but might not be apparent yet in very young birds. If you are uncertain, it is best to ask the salesperson or simply take a canary expert along for the purchase of your bird.

Canaries and Other Pets

As a typical prey animal (one that flees rather than fights), the canary has respect for most other pets. However, there are also canaries that have only a weak *flight instinct*. In an encounter with a cat, that can quickly lead to disaster. The sight of a canary can readily trigger the hunting instinct of a dog or cat, even when the bird is inside a closed cage. These large predators will simply tumble the cage from its position and the bird often escapes, only to be quickly captured by either cat or dog. Therefore, it is best not to expose the canary to such danger. Simply do not let such large animals into the same room where the canary cage is located, or use a ceiling hook to locate the cage safely out of reach. Also be aware of the dangers from snakes and ferrets, which can quickly kill your bird if given the opportunity.

There are rarely ever problems between canaries and rodents such as guinea pigs, rabbits, hares, or hamsters, unless both are kept in the same room at night: When, for instance, the hamster "jogs" all night on its exercise wheel, it will disturb the birds, which normally sleep during the hours of darkness. With tame rats, there is a possibility of bite injuries, so it is advisable not to let both animals run or fly in the same room. Please note that all small mammals, reptiles, and amphibians can harbor bacteria that might sicken or kill your bird, so wash your hands thoroughly before handling the canary or its food or water.

Canaries and Children

Canaries are really suitable only for children who are old enough to understand and appreciate that canaries must always be approached slowly and quietly. Moreover, taking on the responsibility to feed them daily, clean their cage, and engage with them on a daily basis can be too much for young children to handle. In this case, the parents have to accept a fair amount of co-responsibility for the care of the birds.

Yet, canaries are ideal for older children, especially since these birds can become very tame if they are worked with intensively and properly trained. Then it is even possible to teach them to perform small tricks or to have them sit on the shoulder of the children while they are doing their homework. Nevertheless, the children's room is not a suitable location for cage and birds, especially if the child has allergies. The most suitable location for a birdcage is the room where most family activities take place, for instance, in the living room.

The ultimate responsibility for the health and well-being of these little canaries rests with parents, even though the bird may belong to their child.

The Question of **Age**

JUVENILE CANARIES A canary between the age of six to eight months is ideally suitable to start training. At that age, these birds are fully weaned and fledged and are able to feed by themselves.

MOLTING After six months, canaries have completed their first molt. With that behind them they are less susceptible to stress and diseases. The immune system of a canary's body is particularly weakened during the molting period.

SETTLING IN Juvenile birds will adjust more readily to changes than older birds. Therefore, young canaries are easier to settle in and make hand tame. However, this does not mean that older birds are not able to establish an equally close bond with their owner!

A Brief Course in Ornithology

Just as in wild canaries, the body of pet canaries is streamlined, which is particularly conspicuous when canaries are observed in flight. A canary's bones are hollow in order to conserve weight and to facilitate flying. The feathers deteriorate because of wear and tear, and are consequently lost during the molt and replaced with newly grown feathers. When the bird fluffs up its plumage, warm air accumulates between the feathers, and this then regulates the body temperature of the bird. The stout, wedge-shaped beak is perfectly suited for husking seeds, but it is less suited as an aid for climbing. The legs of canaries are long and thin, and the feet have four toes. With these, canaries are able to hold on to branches as well as hop along on the ground.

Discovering the World by Using All Senses

Canaries have extremely good eyesight. They are able to absorb many images in a very short period, even in fast flight. Their hearing is also very well developed, but their senses of smell and taste are less acute than in humans.

Vision Canaries can discriminate between colors very well, because that is the basis of their ability to select food. A red pharyngeal spot in the back of the throat of nestlings signals to the parents that a nestling is hungry. The spot is present only during that stage of life, and is visible only when the beak is opened wide by the begging chick.

Hearing Canaries have well-developed hearing. This is not particularly surprising since males delineate their territory by singing; females select their male partner on the basis of his vocalizing skills.

Sense of smell The sense of smell is not particularly well developed in canaries, since they normally respond to visual cues.

Sense of taste Taste does not play a particularly significant role in the life of canaries, because food is selected principally based on color and consistency. However, canaries do display strong preferences for particular treats, such as dandelion greens, or certain seeds, such as hemp and millet.

Canaries like to play with green feed and examine it for small insects—often spending hours on it!

Anatomy and Senses

Tail

A bird's tail aids steering and balancing in flight, like the rudder on an airplane. It also acts as a brake when the bird is landing. The longer the tail feathers, the more ability a bird has to twist and maneuver in flight. In canaries, the tail is not as long as in some other pet birds, such as parakeets.

Ears

At first glance, the ears are not visible. They are located laterally behind and slightly below the eyes, hidden as small holes among the plumage. If your canary is hand tame and allows you to scratch its head, you can carefully part the feathers to see its ears.

Plumage

The plumage fulfills important tasks in all birds. On one hand, it pro-tects against cold and wetness, and on the other hand, it facilitates flying. The feathers are extremely lightweight and make up only about 8percent of the total body weight. All feathers, including the tail feathers, are replaced during the molting period in late summer or autumn.

Wings

In the wild, wings are the life insurance of canaries. When a bird is perched, the wings are folded closely against the body. In flight, the wingspan of canaries is approxi-mately 9 inches (23 cm). Canaries spend a lot of time caring for their feathers. Various wing positions can be used for communication among the flock.

Eyes

Except for albinos, which have red eyes, the eyes of canaries are black and located laterally alongside the head. This arrangement provides an extremely wide field of vision, which is common in prey species. When in flight, canaries need to absorb and process a large number of images in a short space of time.

Beak

The wedge-shaped beak doesn't assist canaries in climbing, but it can be used very effectively to pick up objects. In a healthy bird, the continuously growing beak should wear down evenly along its entire edge. Illness or injury can cause it to become deformed or overgrown. When that happens, it is difficult or—in extreme cases—impossible for the birds to feed normally. Pet canaries can use cuttlebones or natural branches to grind down their beaks. Alternately, your veterinarian can show you how to trim your canary's beak.

Claws

Canaries have four toes—three are pointing forward and one is pointing backward. If the claws are too long, it is difficult for the birds to hop along so claws must be trimmed properly.

The Canary Home

If canaries are given everything they need, these active little birds are rather undemanding. In essence, the prerequisites for perfect bird happiness are a properly equipped cage, kept in a suitable location and fitted with natural wooden perches, a bathing dish, and lots of love and attention!

What to Consider When Buying a Canary

Anyone who brings a canary into his or her home accepts the responsibility of looking after the bird for 10 or even 15 years. Therefore, you will need to contemplate such an acquisition very carefully, and then take your time when selecting your new housemate. It is advisable to look at birds available from several pet shops and/or canary breeders before you make a final decision.

Where to buy?

Irrespective of whether you purchase the canary from a reputable pet shop (where you can get detailed and competent advice) or from a breeder, do not be rushed into the purchase! Although the first impression (in respect to color and song) is usually the best, you should actually take your time to listen to the bird's singing for a while. It is important that you perceive that bird's song as very pleasant; after all, you will hear it every day for many years to come. Sometimes canaries are available from animal shelters. These birds deserve to have a new home and loving care. Often these facilities also have pairs of canaries that have already been together for a while. Such birds are then easy to integrate into completely new surroundings. Another possibility to acquire a canary is from a bird fair. However, birds at a fair might be stressed and it can be hard to determine their real condition. Yet, the selection available from bird fairs is often quite comprehensive. If you are looking for a particular color variety or would like to compare the song from different varieties, you might have a better opportunity at such an event. In any case, make sure that the particular canary you are focusing on is being properly cared for: Are all the birds for sale being kept in clean cages? Is the cage sufficiently large? Does the food look fresh? Another good sign is when a bird appears curious and actively moves around in the cage.

The Difficulty of Choosing

The best time of day to purchase a canary is in the morning. At that time of day, these birds are at their most active. Observe the particular bird you intend to buy for a while and look for possible disease symptoms or suspicious behavioral characteristics: Limping or constantly sitting in one spot could be signs of an illness or injury. The bird must be able to reach all perches in its cage easily. While making these observations, do not stand too close to the cage, because this could disturb the bird. In potentially dangerous situations, birds often attempt to

appear as normal as possible to remain inconspicuous to a predator. Also, take a close look at the other birds in the same cage. If a bird is sick, it is advisable not to purchase any of the other birds in the same cage, because they too could be infected. In order to be able to recognize the characteristics of a healthy bird, please read the Expert Tip (next page). Once you have decided on a particular bird, asked the salesperson about its sex, age, and possible peculiarities. (For example, perhaps it has a rather characteristic song, has already bred, or is very tame.)

Note: Once the salesperson has caught the bird, have another look at it. Gently touch the breast musculature of the bird to check its weight—it must not have any depressions, and the breastbone (sternum) must not protrude. If the bird is underweight, it could be ill.

How important is the leg band?

Although not mandated by law in many areas, some breeders will fit their canaries with a leg band, which lists the breeder number, year of birth of the bird, and often a consecutive number that identifies the individual bird of a particular clutch of eggs, from a particular female or parents. Make a note of the leg band number of your bird, so that if it ever escapes, you will be able to identify it again. Moreover, make sure that the leg band is not too tight. It should easily spin around the leg.

Shiny plumage, clear eyes, as well as clean legs and vent (cloacal) region; these characteristics identify a healthy bird.

In the event a leg band has become too tight, a veterinarian must remove it.

Transporting Your Pet Home

For taking your new pet home, you will need a carrier or box the size of a shoe box (some pet shops provide carry boxes, but check first). Such a box prevents injuries and protects against drafts. Moreover, most birds will keep calm when they are in the dark. A plastic carrier can also be used later to take the bird to a veterinarian, when necessary. It is important, however, that the box have ventilation slots and a door that is easy to open, so that the bird can be removed quickly. To release your canary at home into its cage, hold the box with its opening against the (open) cage door. Give the bird sufficient time to hop into the cage. Under no circumstances should you shake the bird out of the box.

Preparing the Cage

It is advisable to prepare the cage for your new pet in advance of its arrival. Carefully select a suitable location for the cage. You should measure the proposed space available, so that you will know what size cage to purchase at the pet shop. Not all commercially available cages are suitable for keeping birds in general, and for canaries in particular. Seek the advice of the sales assistant. Also make sure that the cage is properly equipped (see page 24). Fill dishes with seeds, fruit, and water before the bird is released into the cage, so that it can explore the cage undisturbed for hours. It is also advisable to assess—well in advance—the availability and location of an avian veterinarian in your area.

Your Canary's Health at a Glance

TIPS FROM
CANARY EXPERT
Thomas Haupt

PLUMAGE When a bird preens itself regularly, the plumage will be shiny. All feathers should be smooth against the body and there must be no bare patches. Only during the molting period should there be some irregularities noticeable in the plumage. Therefore, it is prudent to purchase a canary after it has completed its molt, sometime in late autumn.

CLOACA AND LEGS The cloaca (vent) region and legs must not be coated with fecal matter, and there must not be encrustations of any kind. Under ideal circumstances, the claws must be short and clean.

EYES AND BEAK Eyes and nostrils must be clear and without discharge. The bird must not be sneezing or making clicking respiratory sounds. The bird's tail should not pump up and down as it breathes, and the breathing should be smooth. The beak must be able to close symmetrically along its entire perimeter; otherwise, it will need to be trimmed frequently later on.

BODY The presence of fatty padding indicates that you are looking at older birds, which are sometimes offered by unscrupulous dealers.

The Feel-Good Home

Canaries need a lot of activity. The more interesting their home setup is, the more active and contented the birds are.

The Ideal Birdcage

Cage sizes of at least 16 inches (40 cm) long, 8 inches (20 cm) wide, and 16 inches (40 cm) high are suitable for one or two birds. The rule of thumb: Birds must be able to—at least—spread and flap their wings inside the cage. Round—as well as narrow and tall— cages are less suitable. Birds prefer to move about in a horizontal environment, so a bird home of a long, rectangular shape is perfect. Beyond

that, it is also ideal to have the wire bars arranged vertically, and the distance between bars should be approximately ½ inch (1.5 cm). A large cage door facilitates daily maintenance work inside the cage.

Finding the Right Location

A suitable cage location is very important, so that your canary remains healthy and active.

> Your canary will be happiest in your home where there is a lot of activity. Canaries need to be provided with adequate stimulation from outside the cage to prevent boredom. However, the birds should also be given an opportunity to withdraw if and when they want to.

> Place the cage securely in an elevated position. Birds feel safer when they have an overview of their surroundings. If the cage is too low, the birds become unsettled, because in the wild, birds of prey approach from above, and predators, such as cats and rats, come from the ground up.

> Place the cage in a well-lit position, preferably in the morning sun, because canaries like to sunbathe occasionally. However, you must also make sure that part of the cage is shaded so that the bird does not become overheated.

> Many bird hobbyists worry that their canaries are exposed to drafts when a window is open, and fear this will have a detrimental effect on the health of their birds. Fresh air is healthy, and a cool breeze for a few minutes will not harm the birds.

Branches, ropes, and swings. These make for an ideal environment for canaries. It gives the birds an opportunity to exercise their wings.

A few pots of herbs and a water dish provide a vitamin-rich in-between snack for these active energy bundles.

A perfect playground can be set up in the bird room with natural branches suspended from the room's ceiling by ropes.

However, having a steady stream of cold air coming in through a window with faulty sealing is not good for your canary.

Pure Luxury: Bird Room and Aviary

Providing canaries with a dedicated bird room or an outside aviary will do the birds a lot of good.

Dedicated bird room Equip such a room with perches, ropes, and branches along the walls and suspended from the ceiling. The floor can be covered with newspaper or a drop cloth. A shelf, raised off the floor, for bathing and food dishes completes the room. Cover the windows with bright curtains or screening. You must clean the bird litter once a week and scrub all branches thoroughly. Remove bird droppings and empty seed husks daily.

Aviary Outdoor aviaries are available ready-made in wood or metal, covered with wire mesh.

To avoid injuries from animals or wild birds, there should be an additional layer of mesh attached to the inside of the frame. If you want to make the aviary habitable during cooler months, you will need to attach plastic film along the outside, before the onset of cold weather. Canaries are tolerant of temperatures down to about 20°F (−8°C), provided they are gradually acclimated and given an opportunity to warm up periodically. It is important to provide an energy-rich diet containing high-fat grains and seeds if the birds are kept outdoors in the cold.

An outdoor aviary should be at least 6 feet (2 m) long and high, and at least 3 feet (1 m) wide.

Caution: Check with your veterinarian or poison control center for a list of poisonous plants before creating an outdoor aviary.

Indoor aviaries are essentially large cages designed for inside use. They are usually made of metal and are commonly available in kit form. A bright, dry basement room, or a corner of a living room are ideally suited for setting up such an aviary.

Basic Equipment for the Canary Home

1 Water Dispenser

To provide your birds with water, you can use a plastic or ceramic dish or stainless steel bowl. However, for hygienic reasons, I recommend the use of a water dispenser.

2 Food Bowls

Birdcages usually come with plastic bowls that can be refilled from the outside of the cage. Yet, because plastics eventually crack, such food dishes can become breeding grounds for bacteria. Food bowls made of ceramic must be glazed. Personally, I always recommend using stainless steel bowls, which are easy to clean (they can even be placed in the dishwasher) and they last a long time. If you have several birds, you should use large bowls. Essentially, you will require two food bowls: one for seeds or pellets and another one for fruit and green feed.

3 Bathing Facility

Because canaries are passionate about baths, you should always have a bathing dish or a birdbath available, or provide a bathing facility during free flight sessions.

4 Bird Grit

Canaries hull their seeds before swallowing them, so they do not require insoluble grit to properly digest food. However, soluble mineral grit, such as ground oyster shell or crushed eggshells, will aid in digestion and provide a valuable source of calcium. Do not use sandpaper perch covers or cage bottom liners, which are rough on the bird's feet and provide no benefit.

5 Perches

Offer perches of variable thicknesses, such as natural branches from untreated nut or fruit trees. This type of perch automatically exercises leg musculature and generally prevents pressure sores. These are available in pet shops, or you can harvest your own. Just be certain to use branches that haven't been exposed to pesticides or car exhaust, and scrub them thoroughly in hot soapy water to remove germs and insects. You can also provide a flat wooden perch or narrow shelf approximately 1 to 1½ inches (3 to 4 cm) wide, which will allow the bird to stand flat and relax its feet. Rope perches made of cotton, hemp, or woven plastic are also popular.

6 Cuttlebones

These soft, natural cuttlefish bones provide an excellent source of calcium, and act as an effective grinding stone for the beak. However, some canaries have difficulty removing pieces from the cuttlefish bone. Ask your veterinarian if an additional calcium supplement is necessary.

Toys for canaries

SWING Canaries are not as playful as parrots, but they do like a swing (which imitates the movement of branches in the wind) in their cage. The birds like to sit on them and even sleep there. Swings improve balance and muscle tone.

TOYS Instead of toys, canaries often prefer to be involved with you, their friend and keeper.

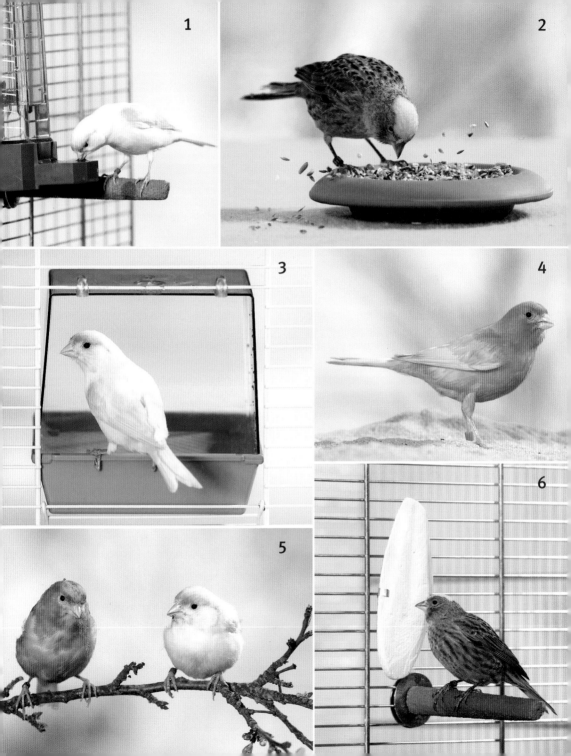

Settling In

The cage has been prepared, and the canary has been brought home. Now the time has come to give your pet sufficient time to adjust to its new surroundings, and for you to gradually—step-by-step—acquaint yourself with your new pet.

The First Few Days . . .

If you observe the following points, your canary will adjust to its new home quickly and with minimal stress.

Peace and quiet After all the excitement of being transported, give your canary a few hours' rest. It is quite possible that the bird will initially react by wildly flapping its wings in response to every sound and movement around the cage (it is trying to "flee"). That is a normal reaction until the bird is used to the household's sights and sounds. Stay as far away from the cage as possible, so that the bird does not perceive you as a threat. Soon it will settle down.

Exploration When the canary starts to preen itself and inspect the cage, it is showing signs of adjustment to the new environment. During the first three or four days give your new friend sufficient time to orient itself.

Free flight Under no circumstances should the canary be allowed out of its cage during this phase! The bird will never return on its own, since it does not yet recognize the cage as its new home. If you do it anyway, you will have to chase the bird, which then could destroy the delicate bonds of the emerging friendship.

Making contacts After a few days the bird will appreciate that you do not represent a threat. At that stage, it will know who brings food and water, and your pet may even start to initiate contact with you. If not, you will have a job cut out for yourself.

Care plan The first step is to condition your canary to a regular schedule for feeding and cage maintenance. This activity firms up your relationship and your bird will start to trust you.

Building confidence Always move slowly when in the proximity of the cage. Sudden movements will unsettle a new bird and it will respond by trying to flee. Once a basis of trust has been established, you can start working toward taming. The curiosity of the canary will do the rest to solidify the relationship with you.

Happy and lively: During the first few days in the new home, every detail is examined with immense curiosity.

Bonding with Your Canary

If you want to have very tame canaries, you must always deal with only one bird at a time. Even if you want to keep several canaries, and have all of them friendly and hand tame, it is best to start out with a single bird. Tame it step-by-step (see below), and only after that bird is tame, purchase a second or even third one. Each new bird must also be tamed first before it can be put together with birds that are already tame. This way distractions are avoided. If after that you continue to interact intensively with your canaries, the initially gained trust will be retained. Also, always remember (not only during the initial phase of the taming process but also later on) that canaries have only a limited attention span and always require appropriate

1 GETTING TO KNOW EACH OTHER Give your canary sufficient time to become familiar with the new surroundings. Stay close by, but keep the cage door closed. Talk to the bird with a calm and relaxed voice. Approach the cage very slowly, step-by-step, but only as far as this does not provoke a flight reaction, until you are finally directly in front of the cage.

2 A LITTLE "TEMPTATION" WILL HELP While talking softly to the bird, place your hand on top of the cage. The bird will soon understand that there is no threat coming from the hand. At that stage, you can tempt the bird with a tasty treat: Maybe you know already what its favorite food is. If so, offer some of it through the wire bars. A spray of millet or other canary treats often prove to be effective.

3 GAINING TRUST If your canary accepts food through the wire, place your hand with the treat clearly visible inside the cage. Make these rewards so small that the bird needs to hop on your hand to reach them. Have patience. During the final step, you can take the bird—while it is sitting on your hand—out of the cage and return it. The reward for this is a tasty treat. Of course, always be certain that windows and doors are securely closed and that other pets are safely shut away.

rest and feeding periods. During these periods, the birds should also be able to completely withdraw, bathe, and preen their plumage or maintain contacts with the other birds. Several small training units per day are better than long sessions that would quickly tire out the bird. In a worst-case scenario, your canary would then relate the training session to something negative.

You should also avoid loud noises, doors slamming, and hammering music as much as possible during the time spent with your bird. Otherwise,

Success! With a bit of patience and a tasty treaty, in this case dandelion greens, you will soon attract the bird to sit on your hand.

you will scare the bird and it will fly away to seek cover. However, canaries will adapt relatively quickly to repetitive sounds, which will then no longer be considered as threatening, such as the use of the vacuum cleaner in the vicinity of the birdcage. Eventually this will no longer present a problem, but you should not start out by vacuuming in the immediate vicinity of the cage; instead work your way gradually from the door of the room towards the cage.

Strengthening the Bond

The first steps on the way to a lifelong friendship with your canary have been taken. If you now observe the following points and do not force a bird to do anything it does not want to do, you can further fortify and strengthen its trust in you.

Strong-willed Canaries are not cuddle toys and they have their own minds. Do not squeeze the bird too hard and do not hold it too firmly in your hand; otherwise, the bird will quickly associate that with something negative. Let the bird move away when it wants to.

Running your fingers through the bird's feathers Canaries like having that done to them along their abdominal region, but only after they have gained confidence and trust in you. Most do not like to be touched along their back, but maybe your bird is an exception. Try it and find out.

Caves Although canaries are curious and will explore all hollows and cavelike locations, they do not like to be put in your coat or pants pockets. Similarly, they do not like to crawl under clothing.

Treats Reward your canary for a behavior you are trying to encourage. The bird will remember that and repeat the behavior in order to get another treat (positive reinforcement).

Fitness Through Food

To be as lightweight as possible for efficient flying, canaries do not carry substantial body reserves around with them. Their plumage simulates a greater body mass than these birds actually have. Their metabolism operates constantly at its peak, because the normal body temperature is already about 107°F (42°C). Consequently, canaries have considerable energy requirements. In order for canaries to always meet their minimum body requirements, a diverse and well-balanced diet is vital. Keep in mind that less-active caged birds will require less energy than their wild counterparts, so adjust the diet according to your pet's activity level.

Seeds as Principal Food

The principal food source for canaries is a balanced diet of seeds, which are readily available from pet shops. A high-quality mix should be made up of various seeds, for instance rapeseed, canary seed, linseed, millet, oat groat, hemp, or niger (thistle)

A spray of millet, together with parsley, is a special treat for canaries. Because millet is very carbohydrate-rich, it should not be on the menu every day.

seed. Food quality is very important for the health of all birds. Make sure that the seeds for your canary look shiny and do not smell musty. All food items should have an intense color; for instance, rapeseeds must be red, millet yellowish, poppy seeds black. Inclusions, such as bits of soil and empty seed husks, as well as signs of mold or fungus, are an indication of inferior quality. Unfortunately, mold and fungus are sometimes nearly impossible to detect, so pick a high-quality mix from a reputable manufacturer.

Storage Do not buy too much food ahead of time, since it can become rancid. Keep it dry and cool in an airtight plastic container. Seed mix can be kept for several weeks, provided it does not get moist or—worse—wet; you should always smell it before feeding it to your birds. Seed can be kept in the refrigerator or freezer to prolong the shelf life, but be cautious if you later decide to switch to room temperature for further storage, as the moisture (sweat) from the refrigerated mix can lead to the development of mold and fungi. Either keep it in the fridge, or place it in a well-ventilated container to allow the moisture to dissipate before sealing up. Also, keep in mind that birdseed on sale in large chain stores could have been in storage for some time, which can lead to a deterioration of quality (loss of vitamin content). It is best to purchase canary food from pet shops, and check for "best by" dates now in use by some manufacturers.

Favorite food Many canaries have a favorite seed, which they eat to the exclusion of other seeds. Often, such favorites are particularly fatty seeds, which—in the long term—can make canaries fat. However, it is virtually impossible to train a bird to eat all types of seeds given. Moreover, starving such a bird until it eats all the seeds from a single bowl can be very damaging. Therefore, you should experiment with different mixes until you find one that your canary enjoys and eats well.

Diversity is recommended Winter food for canaries that live in an outdoor aviary should contain more fatty seeds such as oats or hemp. These particular seeds can be periodically added to the all-purpose seed mixture. Similarly, other seeds offered separately, such as various millets, oats, parakeet seeds, or a twig of millet spray enrich the seed diet and keep your bird interested. The key is to provide nutritional diversity.

Fruits and vegetables are quickly turned into toys, just like this little "tower." This type of food should always be offered in "beak size" pieces!

Various herbs and salad greens can make a tasty treat. These foods can give your bird the necessary vitamin "boost" needed for their healthy lifestyle.

Not only pretty to look at, but also very tasty: Buds and flowers from fruit trees that have not been sprayed with chemicals can enrich the dietary plan of your birds.

Vitamins Through Green Feed

Fruits and vegetables Green feed contains important vitamins and minerals that are absent from seeds. You should give fresh fruit, such as apples, pears, grapes, mangoes, kiwifruit, cherries, berries, dates, figs, or even a banana, all cut into beak-size pieces. Some of the more popular vegetables are carrots, beets, kohlrabi, radishes, or boiled potatoes. If possible, these should be given as organic foods since they are not sprayed with insecticides and are free of chemical contaminants. If you can't feed organic, make sure to scrub any produce thoroughly before offering it to your pet.

Keeping active while feeding Apple slices, pieces of carrot, or small chunks of beets can—for the sake of diversity—be wedged onto a branch or between wire bars, so that the birds can pick on them as desired.

Greens and herbs You can also offer green lettuce, dandelion leaves, daisies, chickweed, parsley and ribwort (plantain), as well as the seeds of wild grasses, to provide further dietary diversity.

Formulated Diets

Another option for adding variety and high-quality nutrition to your canary's diet is to offer some formulated food. Formulated (pelleted or extruded) diets have been used for a few decades for pet birds. Most bird keepers refer to these diets simply as "pellets," even though the majority today are actually extruded. No matter what you call them, these diets blend a mix of ground cooked grains, vitamins, minerals,

---

How to feed correctly

BE REGULAR Always feed at specific times.

FRESH Food rations must be prepared fresh every day.

HYGIENE Remove any uneaten fruit and vegetables every evening.

QUANTITIES Offer sufficient food so that the birds are not hungry. Seeds: every day, 1—2 tablespoons per bird.

and sometimes probiotics into a small, flavorful (and usually colorful) morsel. They are as nutritionally complete as modern avian feed research allows. Some birds love pellets, whereas others shun them. If you introduce your canary to this healthy dietary staple at a young age, and consistently offer a small separate dish or mix some in with the seed, your bird will probably grow to accept and even relish the treat.

Calcium Supplements

Fine-grain shell grit provides a valuable source of calcium for your pet. It is advisable to mix some soluble grit (for example, ground oyster shell) in with the regular seed mix, which then provides the required supply of calcium. Sometimes, the birds will also enjoy a bowl filled with organic potting soil, with a small patch of grass planted in it. This will provide additional vitamins and minerals.

Water is life's elixir. It needs to be replaced daily. When you are using an open drinking bowl that too needs to be checked regularly for bird droppings and food particles, and cleaned as required.

Protein Makes Strong Birds

Canaries will benefit occasionally from animal proteins as an additional energy booster. You can purchase manufactured rearing food mixtures or egg food mixtures, available from your pet shop. You can also make your own egg food by hard-boiling an egg, and then mashing it (shell and all, for a calcium boost) together with finely ground-up carrots or an apple. Such calorie-rich food should be given only occasionally to nonbreeding birds; otherwise, your pet will become overweight.

Water

Fresh, clean water is critical for your bird's health. If you are offering drinking water in an open bowl your pet might use it as a bathtub. Change the water at least daily, preferably twice a day in warm weather. Otherwise, there will be a rapid development of bacteria in the water, which can readily lead to diseases. Change the drinking water in dispenser tubes daily as well.

Caution: toxic!

> Any green parts of tomatoes or potatoes, raw potatoes, green beans, avocado, plums, and grapefruit are inedible for canaries and must not be offered as food.

> Your bird should not be permitted to nibble on houseplants, even when they are considered nontoxic. Instead, keep a supply of fresh greens available.

> Branches from yew trees, Laburnum, and Liguster (wild privet) must never be used as part of a cage setup and decoration, because of their toxicity. Always be sure that any branches are safe and clean before offering them to your bird.

How to Keep Your Canaries Happy

The successful recipe for a great relationship between humans and birds is as follows: patiently establish trust, and provide an appealing cage, plenty of exercise and stimulation, lots of love, and a balanced diet.

What to do

(+) Establish contact with your canaries during the first few days by softly talking to them.

(+) Locate the cage in an elevated position in a room where there is a lot of activity. The birds will feel safe there and have a good overview of the entire room.

(+) Feed at regular times and provide a diverse yet balanced diet. This will keep these active little birds contented.

(+) Right from the start you should make ample time available for your birds. Make sure there is plenty to keep your pet occupied, such as a swing, a bowl with planted grass, or a millet spray, which the bird can pick apart at its leisure.

What not to do

(−) Do not allow the birds out of their cage during the first few days; otherwise you will need to spend a lot of effort chasing and catching them.

(−) Avoid sudden movements and loud music in the vicinity of the cage.

(−) Do not make sudden dietary changes; the birds will need to adjust gradually to all types of green feed. Do not offer any unfamiliar plants as food.

(−) Do not force a canary to do anything it does not want to do. Be patient during the taming period and use a reward rather than punishment system.

Health and Maintenance

Because canaries' plumage is of vital importance to their survival, they spend many hours every day preening their feathers and putting them neatly back into their respective positions. Apart from providing appropriate accommodations and a suitable diet, you will also need to support the well-being of your birds by performing appropriate daily maintenance tasks and closely monitoring your canaries to see whether they are indeed doing well.

Basic Necessities for a Long Bird Life

Our canaries will spend nearly their entire life in a cage or an aviary. However, unlike birds in the wild, our pets can't escape if their environment is fouled. It is up to you to keep things clean and safe. Contaminated drinking water is a breeding ground for bacteria, and dirty perches allow your pet to track fecal contaminants and spoiled food into water and food dishes. Therefore, regular cage maintenance is part of the daily servicing routine that must be done. In essence, this includes thoroughly cleaning food and water bowls (including the drink dispenser), changing cage bottom paper, removing all uneaten food, and wiping down perches.

Prevention is Critical

Canaries can reach an age of up to 15 years, but only if they are lovingly cared for so that they remain healthy. A very important aspect here is a well-balanced diet that provides the birds with appropriate nutrients and vitamins but without supplying too much food (see pages 31/32) that could make the birds fat. Similarly important is daily interaction with you, which will prevent boredom and help keep them active and fit.

You must also keep the "mind" of these active little birds fit, by offering a lot of different activities (see pages 50/55). Moreover, you need to make sure to avoid stress factors such as other pets poking at the cage or loud noises. The daily cage maintenance also serves as a way for you to check whether your bird appears healthy or whether it appears withdrawn. That could be the first sign of the onset of a disease. It gives you the opportunity to intervene quickly with appropriate measures, such as an immediate visit to the veterinarian.

Caring for Canaries Made Easy

In order to be able to fly away quickly in the wild, the plumage of canaries must be fully deployable at any time. Moreover, it protects the birds against wind, rain, and cold weather. Therefore, it is very important for these active little birds to have their feathers cleaned, preened, and in top condition at all times.

Preening the Plumage

Canaries preen their feathers in various stages (several times a day) and with total dedication. Here the beak plays an important role: Not only is it used for eating, drinking, and to carry nesting material, but it is the single most important tool for preening. Since the beak is relatively sensitive, canaries need to care for it constantly.

› Individual feathers are pulled through the beak one by one, removing small dirt particles and dust.
› Since large bird feathers are structurally similar to a zipper, the bird also checks whether the cross "braces" still fit properly into each other, and whether the streamlined appearance of the plumage is maintained. If that is not the case, flying will become difficult for the bird and the insulating properties of the plumage will be impeded, which can lead to a loss of body heat.

Protection Against Rain and Loss of Body Heat

To make the feathers water resistant, the bird will rub its beak against a preen gland located at the base of its tail. The oily secretions from this gland are then worked into the feathers during preening, which keeps them shiny and pliable. Once applied to the feathers, this smooth surface coat will readily repel water, and cold air cannot easily penetrate beneath the feathers. At the same time, air warmed by body heat is retained under the plumage, which keeps the bird warm on cold days.

Preventing Diseases

Since your pet will spend a great deal of time grooming, it's important that you keep its environment as clean as possible. Otherwise, pathogens in the cage can end up on your pet's feathers, and then in its beak as it preens, which can lead to disease. Therefore, you must always keep perches and the cage bottom clean. Be careful when arranging perches so that your canary does not have the ability to foul other perches or food and water dishes because of the positioning of the perch. Always offset them sufficiently to prevent cross contamination.

Mutual **Preening**

OBSERVATION If you are keeping a bonded pair of canaries, you will occasionally observe that the birds preen each other.

REASON Mutual preening fosters social bonding and reduces stress. However, canaries are not as socially inclined, as—for instance—parrots are.

BATHING Canaries love water. If you place tepid water in a bowl inside the cage, you will need to change the cage-bottom paper after the bath; otherwise, it becomes a breeding ground for germs. Birdbaths are available that can be suspended from the inside of a cage door. These are very popular, and keep the mess somewhat contained. Similarly, wet lettuce leaves are often enthusiastically accepted as a substitute. Many birds will roll around among the wet leaves, which in essence is a form of preening the plumage. For that, you must use only leaves that have not been sprayed with insecticides.

CLEANING FEATHERS The bird is pulling each feather repeatedly through its beak, to arrange the plumage properly and to remove any dirt. At the same time, parasites are being removed. Apart from the beak, legs and toes also become involved in this activity. In the wild, a healthy plumage is vital, and therefore, preening has the highest priority in the daily maintenance routine of canaries.

BEAK The bird will remove encrustations of soft food along the edges of the beak by rubbing the material off onto a perch. Therefore, you will need to check periodically whether the beak is growing evenly on all sides.

A Matter of Cleanliness

Although cage hygiene is important, it is virtually impossible to keep birds completely germ-free. Moreover, a certain degree of immune stimulation through exposure to microorganisms can be beneficial in building a strong immune system, in humans and in animals. Nevertheless, regular cleaning and proper hygiene will help keep harmful pathogens to a manageable level.

Daily Cage Maintenance

A few small maintenance tasks must be performed every day. To get this done efficiently, it helps if the birds are accustomed to your hand.

Fecal material Fecal material should be removed from perches and bars. Cage bottoms should be cleaned and substrate changed. You can use plain newsprint, or one of the many bird-safe substrates available in pet stores.

Bowls Remove all uneaten fruit and vegetables from food and bathing bowls, as well as leftover

water from the drink dispenser. These items should be thoroughly washed out and allowed to dry completely before they are refilled and returned to the cage. It helps to have two sets of dishes, so that there is always a clean set ready to service the cage.

Birds While you are performing these maintenance tasks, your canary can enjoy a free flight, provided other pets are locked away and all hazards are removed.

Major Maintenance Tasks

Major maintenance on cage and equipment should be scheduled for at least once a week:

Cage Clean the cage thoroughly with water and a gentle dish detergent or other bird-safe soap, and rinse and dry thoroughly. This procedure can also be applied to perches, where a hand brush comes in handy. Clean any toys or swings, and wash them in hot water. Dishes and plastic items can be run through the dishwasher if you prefer. Place a fresh layer of newspaper or other substrate in the cage bottom.

Bowls Clean all dishes, including water bowl or water dispenser, seed dishes, and fresh food dishes in hot soapy water, or run through the dishwasher. Air-dry all items before you refill them and return them to the cage.

Room At least once a week you should vacuum the floor around the cage. If the room has a carpet, consider shampooing it at least once a year.

Wet cage substrate is a potential breeding ground for bacteria. Please replace daily!

Do not forget Always check the seed supply for freshness. Discard any that smells musty or rancid. Perches should be replaced with new ones as needed. Replacement perches are widely available at pet shops, and come in a wide array of materials. Plastic or smooth wood perches can even be cleaned in the dishwasher along with the food and water dishes. Be aware that plastic or ceramic containers that are cracked can harbor microorganisms that could possibly transmit pathogens to your birds. Discard these as they become worn and cracked.

My tip It is very practical to have a duplicate set of food and water containers, so that one set can be cleaned and dried while the other set is in use.

Cleaning Agents—but Which Ones?

Do not use any harsh chemical agents. The fumes from these are harmful to the sensitive respiratory systems of birds and can even kill your pet. Similarly, disinfectants are also unnecessary unless you are fighting a known pathogen or disease outbreak. Use them under the advice of your veterinarian, and follow directions carefully.

Two-Minute Health Check

› Is the bird active and interested in its surroundings?
› Are its eyes and nostrils clear and without discharge?
› Is the cloaca clean and without soiled or pasted feathers?
› Is the plumage smooth and without bare patches?
› Brief and occasional lethargy might be caused by tiredness, but when a canary is constantly listless, it is best to take the bird to a veterinarian immediately.

Cleaning Plan

FOLLOW THE CHECKLIST AND
YOUR PET'S CAGE WILL SHINE!

DAILY	Empty, clean, and refill all food and water containers. That also applies to the bathing bowl. Remove and replace newspaper cover on cage floor. Remove any dirty items. Remove food remnants and fecal material from cage bars and perches. Sticky material can readily be removed with paper towels; subsequently clean everything with a damp cloth. Dried-up bird droppings can easily be vacuumed.
WEEKLY	You will need to vacuum up all feathers around the cage. Periodically offer different toys and change the arrangement of branches in the cage every few weeks. Wash out the cage with soap and scrub everything, including the perches, with a coarse brush. If need be, put bowls in the dishwasher.
MONTHLY	Check ropes, swings, and all perches that they are securely attached. Remove all sharp edges and corners. Check plastic containers for cracks. Wash cage thoroughly under hot, running water.
EVERY THREE MONTHS	It is advisable to replace all old branches that can no longer be cleaned with garden-fresh ones.

Keeping Your Birds Healthy

Canaries are one of nature's little wonders: Despite their high body temperature and rapid metabolism, they have a relatively long life span of 10 to 15 years. That is a considerable achievement for such a small animal. On the other hand, canaries have very little systemic reserves and will always attempt to hide that they may be sick, in order not to attract the attention of predators. Therefore, whenever you detect symptoms of a disease or notice a loss of weight in your birds, always seek the advice of a veterinarian immediately.

Prevention

To avoid diseases in the first place, it is important to enhance the immune defenses of the birds by maintaining hygiene and feeding a well-balanced diet. Also provide your canaries with sufficient fun and physical activity. Make sure to provide plenty of light and fresh air, but avoid drafts.

There are also plant-based preparations and supplements that are designed to stimulate the immune system of birds. These preparations are most effectively used whenever there is increased susceptibility to stress, for example during the molting period or when you are introducing new birds. Beyond that, vitamin preparations, used once or twice a week, support the health of your canaries. These preparations should be used in drinking water according to instructions provided. However, these supplements should not take the place of a healthy diet and a clean cage.

Stress Can Weaken the Immune System During the Molting Period

The molting period, which occurs once a year between late summer and early autumn, is a particularly stressful period for your canaries. The birds are more susceptible to diseases then than at any other time. The molt is triggered by changes in daylight

This is the correct way to hold a canary to administer medication.

A sick canary is often listless and keeps itself away from the other birds. It attempts to retain body heat by fluffing up its plumage.

Once a year, old feathers are shed during the molting period. At that time, supplemental vitamins might be necessary to keep your pet healthy.

hours, which tends to affect hormonal production in birds. Therefore, it is important that the cage be located near a window: Natural daylight in a normal day/night rhythm is the best guarantee for regular progress of the molt. Old and damaged feathers are then lost and replaced by new ones. Initially, all feathers become loose and then fall out on their own or are pulled out by the bird using its beak. New feathers will start up and penetrate the skin. During that period, canaries are often somewhat listless and lethargic. You must not mistake this condition for a legitimate illness, but you will need to be alert so that a disease cannot become established. Support your birds with appropriate diet and supplements as recommended by your veterinarian.

How to Recognize Disease Symptoms

Birds will usually display illness only when they feel that they are not being watched. Therefore, it is advisable not to inspect them at too close a range during cage maintenance, but to still watch them— inconspicuously—from a distance. Healthy and sick birds can usually be distinguished based on clear symptoms:

Healthy birds Healthy birds preen themselves a lot, are active, and always explore their surroundings. Male canaries often sing for hours. Birds that are contented will feed several times during the day. They also like to bathe extensively. After the bath, the birds

Quick Help for **Sick Birds**

CONSULT A VETERINARIAN Whenever a bird becomes sick, a veterinarian should always be consulted.

ACT QUICKLY Do not wait too long; otherwise, the bird may be so weak that it can no longer be treated effectively.

FIRST AID Certain first aid measures can be initiated at home.

will rearrange their feathers, which are then nice and shiny. If you are keeping several canaries, there may occasionally be arguments about particular pieces of food or the position on a swing or branch. A healthy canary sleeps on the highest branch in the cage. When sleeping, he sits on one leg and retracts its head among the plumage. A healthy canary is curious, and will quickly investigate and often nibble on any new items added to the cage.

Sick canaries Here the situation is different: At the onset of a disease, canaries will often sit— near normal—on a perch. They will still attempt to react to events around them. However, when they become weak, such birds usually sit on the floor with heavily fluffed up plumage. They also sleep a lot. Sick birds hardly ever sing and finally stop singing altogether. Many sick birds retreat and sit in a corner where they have a bit more peace. They will no longer preen themselves, and the plumage can take on an unkempt appearance; it may possi-

bly even be sticky or outright dirty. Often the eyes are glued shut or a secretion is discharged from the nostrils. A bird in this condition is critically ill, and requires prompt veterinary attention.

Depending on the disease, the affected birds will stop feeding or will feed excessively and frequently. The feces often change in appearance. They might change color or consistency. Sometimes, the region around the cloaca becomes smeared with fecal matter. All these symptoms are clear alarm bells, and you should always be on the lookout for them.

However, it is also essential that you know the healthy (normal) behavior of your canaries, so that you will recognize any deviations from it. This will give you sufficient time to initiate appropriate corrective action. Sick canaries tend to lose weight rapidly, since canaries have hardly any fat reserves in the first place. When such birds then also stop eating, this deteriorates quickly into a life-threatening condition. Therefore, do not wait around for too long, or your pet will probably not survive. Because canaries are such small patients they are more difficult to treat than, for instance, dogs or cats. The examination alone or the administration of medications often causes enormous stress to canaries because they are not accustomed to such physical handling. The fitter a canary is under such circumstances, the better its chances of recovery are.

"Sick Bay"

If you are keeping several canaries, it is advisable to remove a sick bird immediately and place it into a separate cage. Once in isolation, the bird can relax and not be harassed by others. Be aware that any cagemates of the sick bird have been exposed to the pathogen and might require treatment as well, even if they appear healthy. Relocate the

Light from a heat lamp can help this little patient conserve body heat, which can speed up recovery.

cage to a quiet, warm location and check on the patient frequently. Every "bird household" must have a heat lamp or heating pad. Sick birds will expend a lot of energy trying to maintain their body temperature, so supplemental heat can be a lifesaver. Position the heat lamp so that the heat on your hand held in the proximity of the cage feels pleasantly warm, not extremely hot. You can also drape a heating pad set to low or medium over part of the cage. Always expose only half of the cage to the radiant heat, and allow the other half of the cage to provide a retreat for the bird when it feels too warm. A towel or some similar material must shade this area. This also calms down the bird. The heat lamp can be left on day and night; it is not harmful to the bird. However, be sure there is no possibility of a fire breaking out.

What Can I Do?

Molting problems It can happen that their own, newly formed feathers penetrating the skin sometimes injure canaries. The only time when feathers have blood vessels in the feather shaft is during the early growth period. Damage to feathers at that stage can cause almost constant slight bleeding. It is possible to pull out such a damaged feather with a quick pull on the quill, using a pair of forceps or tweezers. Some iodine ointment should be put on the small hole that has been created by the removal of the feather.

Diarrhea Diarrhea in a bird is usually symptomatic of severe illness, and you should consult a veterinarian as soon as possible, because the affected bird is losing a lot of liquid and minerals. Some foods will cause loose droppings that resemble diarrhea, but this is usually transient and not

---

Visiting the **Veterinarian**

TIPS FROM
CANARY EXPERT
Thomas Haupt

THE RIGHT VETERINARIAN It is advisable to find out the name and location of a veterinarian who specializes in companion birds while your birds are still healthy. Not all veterinarians are skilled at dealing with birds. Write down the emergency telephone number.

PREPARATION If your bird is sick, write down the details about the little patient's behavior, as well as any related questions that you may want to ask the veterinarian. If at all possible, take along a fecal sample for examination by the veterinarian.

TRANSPORTATION Transport the sick bird in a small cardboard or shoe box with ventilation holes. Make sure to handle the box gently during transport, and keep it warm.

MEDICATIONS Make notes of dosages to be given and the duration of the treatment period. Stick to it, because if a dosage is insufficient, it will delay healing. Moreover, do not terminate treatment prematurely even when your canary appears to have been cured. There is always the possibility of a relapse.

accompanied by other symptoms. The white component in fecal matter is the birds' urate. If this changes color to yellow or green, it indicates severe infection. Contact your veterinarian immediately.

Beak and claws If these grow too long, they must be trimmed or the bird is at risk of injury or eating difficulties. It is advisable to have the veterinarian show you how to do that.

Medications and How to Administer Them

When you administer medications via drinking water, you will always run the risk that the bird might not drink enough, and may not ingest the required dosage. Therefore, it is better to hold the canary gently but firmly in your hand (see illustration on page 40) and then drip the prescribed

medication from a small syringe (without needle) directly into the beak. You will need to do this slowly; otherwise, the medication may go down the wrong way. This procedure should be done as quickly but deliberately as possible in order to minimize stress on the bird. If you are right-handed, take the bird in your left hand. Place your hand completely around the body of the bird but without undue pressure. To administer the medication, the bird's head should be held firmly between your index finger and thumb. Then you can insert the tip of the syringe into the beak with your right hand. Another proven method is having one person hold the canary and another person administer the medication. If you are uncertain about this procedure, your veterinarian will no doubt gladly show you how to restrain a bird firmly in your hand.

The Most Common **Canary Diseases**

SYMPTOMS	POSSIBLE CAUSES	POSSIBLE TREATMENT
Cloaca is encrusted with fecal matter, or feathers are pasted with droppings	Digestive impairment, diarrhea, possible kidney problem, viral, fungal, or bacterial infection	Consult a veterinarian for diagnosis. Possible antibiotic or fungal medication required.
Enlargement around vent opening or along lower abdomen in female bird	Egg binding (the female is unable to expel an egg)	Consult a veterinarian; heat lamp, humid heat, surgical or pharmacological intervention if required
Chirping or squeaking respiratory sounds	Mites in air sac, foreign body in respiratory passages	Consult a veterinarian to establish cause; possible mite medication
Discharge from eyes or nostrils	Bacterial or viral infection	Consult a veterinarian to establish particular pathogen for treatment.
Scaly skin along the legs and under the plumage, reddening and itching	Molting (hormonal imbalance), feather parasites, mites	Consult a veterinarian for specific cause; light therapy, mite medication as indicated

Caring for an Aged Bird

The situation with old or very old canaries is similar to that of sick birds—they too require special care and attention.

Make Life Easier for "Senior" Canaries

When you are keeping a canary, you will not need to expect any definitive signs of old age in your bird for a long time. Although older canaries are often somewhat quieter than young birds, they will still actively participate in life in the cage or aviary. However, some birds will get minor joint problems and no longer be able to fly as much as young birds. At that stage the cage or aviary should be fitted with thicker (wider) perches that make it easier for these birds to rest on. Moreover, if you reduce the distances between perches, the canaries will be able to hop from one to the other with greater ease. Give your special attention to these canary "seniors":

> Are they being chased by other canaries in the cage or aviary?

> Are they getting enough food and water?

> Are they losing condition; for example, they can hardly fly or they only hop along the floor?

> Are they withdrawing more and more?

Sometimes, it makes a lot of sense to provide a separate cage for older canaries, where it is easier for them to withdraw and where they have regular access to food. Provide for maximum peace and quiet for such birds.

When the Canary Passes Away

The approaching end of the life expectancy of canaries usually announces itself. Older birds will get age-related health problems that make life sooner or later unbearable for them: A tumor or arthritis can develop, where the legs become swollen so that they no longer support the weight of the bird, which then is often seen lying on the cage floor. Similarly, when a bird no longer feeds and drinks, the end is usually in sight. In such cases, you have to be aware of your responsibility and have the bird's suffering terminated by a veterinarian. At that stage, it is not fair to the bird to wait until it can no longer feed. In nature, a predator would no doubt eat such a bird, sooner rather than later, and well before the onset of any suffering. The trip to the veterinarian and the good-bye are always difficult. However, when a canary has brought you a lot of pleasure over the years, you should not expose it to prolonged suffering at the end of its life span.

Older canaries often withdraw from the activities in a cage. They require a more peaceful environment than younger birds.

Care and Activities

In nature, canaries are constantly exposed to new challenges during their search for food. So that your diminutive pets will not become bored in your home, provide them with plenty of attention and offer ways for them to forage. A spray of millet is a healthy treat, and you can hang it from the cage ceiling so that your pet must hang from the spray as it eats.

Keeping Busy Is Important

In a canary cage, food and water are usually available in excess. Therefore, the bird hardly spends any time searching for food, nor does it need to be particularly imaginative to find food. Moreover, commercially available foods are usually more nutritious than grass seeds in the wild, for which wild canaries often have to search intensely and fly for long distances every day. Consequently, activity and diversity are clearly limited for canaries under cage conditions. If, on top of that, you keep only a single bird and then do not spend much time with it, this can lead to boredom and behavioral impairment. For instance, the bird may constantly hop up and down on the same perch, to burn off excess energy. It may also start pulling out its own feathers. In the wild, canaries often search for food alone and do not maintain close bonds, as is common among parakeets, yet they need to be talked to as well as kept busy to lead a contented life. Therefore, spend as much time as possible with your pet, or consider keeping multiple birds.

Need Attention?

Canaries are quite compatible with each other, except during the breeding season, when nest-building activities or territorial defense takes over. If you are keeping a single pet bird in a typical pet cage, your canary will depend on you for companionship. Keep the cage in a room where the family gathers often—this will allow the canary to feel that it is part of the "flock." While you read or watch television, your bird can chatter and sing to you, and it will appreciate your occasional acknowledgment and attention.

Who with Whom?

If you decide to keep multiple canaries, you'll need to know the sex of the birds. Keeping one male together with several females rarely ever presents any problems. A male and a female kept together as a pair will work very well, but you'll likely end up with baby canaries at some point. Males among themselves might fight to establish territories, and may need to be separated. Females are distinctly less aggressive, except during the breeding season, when there can be some minor fighting. The basic rule is as follows: The more room and avoidance opportunities are available, the better the social integration among canaries.

"Will we become friends?" Maybe not, but canaries are very compatible and usually get along very well with most finches.

A Large Bird Community

Canaries get along very well with other small bird species, for instance with Gouldian Finches. Most of these different species do not get individually involved with each other; if at all, maybe closely related species such as canaries interact with goldfinches or zebra finches. However, under aviary conditions, male goldfinches will fight with canaries for territory. Often a hierarchy develops among these different species, which is then more likely to prevent the establishment of contacts. If you keep several bird species together with canaries, you will need to monitor the birds carefully. Do not place canaries with small parrots such as cockatiels. Even though they might appear compatible, the relatively defenseless canary is helpless against the strong hooked bill of even the smallest parrot.

Additions to the Canary Family

If you want to keep multiple canaries, start out with a single bird and proceed to tame it. Then, a few weeks later, you can buy an additional bird. This way the birds become very friendly with you, and you will remain the most important contact person for them. Alternatively, you can buy several canaries at the same time and release them jointly into the new bird home. Under such conditions, the environment is strange simultaneously for all birds and there will hardly be any aggression. If there are birds already present in the cage and if they have established territories, introduce the new birds as follows:
› Quarantine the new arrivals for the period of time suggested by your veterinarian to ensure they are healthy.
› After quarantine, place the new birds for a few days in a separate cage, adjacent to the main cage.

"We belong together!" Outside the breeding season, canaries are quite contented within a small flock. Prerequisite: The cage must be sufficiently large so that the birds can avoid each other when there are arguments and territorial fights.

> Change the layout inside the main cage. This will dissolve old territories. Also, provide an additional food dish for the new birds.
> Introduce the new birds into the main cage late in the afternoon—when the nocturnal rest period is not far away.
> Initially, watch the birds closely so that you will be able to separate them in case of fighting.

Forming a **Pair**

It is advisable to establish bonded pairs well before or after the breeding season. This way the birds have time to get used to each other and the male will not immediately start to court the female. Two females should be introduced to each other preferably outside the breeding season in autumn or winter.

Understanding Canaries

Canaries express their mood and well-being principally by means of sound and body language. On one hand, they communicate with other canaries, and on the other hand, they communicate with you, their owner—that is, provided you understand the language of canaries.

Body Language of Canaries

Current canary varieties have retained some of the types of behavior of their wild ancestors:

› When a canary is contented, its feathers are flush against the body. Birds that are sick, sleepy, cold, or recently bathed will fluff up their plumage so that warm body heat accumulates between the feathers and the skin.

› Communication with other canaries is principally by means of wing positions: When wings are raised off the body among adult birds, it is generally a threat behavior. On the other hand, juveniles use this posture when begging for food.

› When two birds are facing each other with bodies erect and beaks wide open, the "issue" is generally about food. Both birds want to appear larger than the other one in order to drive off the competitor.

› When two males meet, they will initially sing to each other. Should they then threaten each other,

"That belongs to me!" Erect and with wings spread, this bird defends its water supply.

"This is my branch!" The red bird, with its beak wide open, indicates that the presence of the other bird is not desired.

a mock fight is not very far away. However, before that actually happens, one of them will usually retreat and fly away. If not, canaries will defend their territory using their beaks. Sometimes, a hand reaching into the cage will be attacked in the same manner.

› Occasionally you will observe in bonded pairs that the birds "bill and coo" or even engage in mutual preening, whereby one partner pulls the feathers of the other through its beak. This is considered a particularly intimate display of affection and trust.

Singing and Other Sounds

The virtuoso singing of canaries does not consist only of a single phrase; the singer can also vary the song. Some varieties, such as the Hartz Roller, sing rather softly and melodically, whereas others, such as the Belgian Bult, are able to vocalize rather loudly. Canaries use their singing to mark their territorial claims, as well as for courting a female. If you have two or more males together, the birds sometimes encourage each other with ever intensifying singing. Sometimes this leads to a real competition.

Apart from singing, these bouncy little birds can also give off other sounds for communicating with each other.

Threatening sounds These are emitted during fighting or in competition for food and sounds more piercing than the melodic whistling for which canaries are known. At the same time, the birds open their beaks in a threatening manner.

Contact sounds If a canary calls a partner or another canary, they use so-called contact sounds, like soft whispering. When this is exchanged between partners, it takes on clearly affectionate overtones. If your bird has formed a close bond

With soft brooding sounds the female strengthens its bond to the male, who—in return—supplies the female with food.

with you, the contact sounds can also be directed at you. This could be simply to call you or to show you that the bird enjoys your company. In such a case, the sounds are more like an extended twittering, something like "dee, dee, dee."

Brooding sounds These are usually softer and more delicate. There is also chirping and whispering between male and female, which strengthens the pair bond.

Begging sounds Nestlings emit characteristically demanding begging sounds, which are to persuade the parents to provide food.

Warning sounds When danger is approaching, parent canaries will give off warning sounds that make the nestlings huddle down in the nest in order to avoid discovery by a predator. Fully fledged juveniles will remain motionless or will hide when the parents give off this sound.

Friendship with Humans

Because of their innate curiosity and love of adventure, no day is like any other for canaries. For instance, some birds like to check out open drawers and closets during a free flight session, or they might investigate new furniture items in the room. Although canaries are not quite as playful as parakeets, the more you get involved with your pets and the more stimulation you provide, the tamer and more contented they will become. Consequently,

your canaries will love to become more and more involved with you. If you are keeping a single bird, it will require even more personal involvement and diversity than birds kept in a flock, which are readily distracted by the other birds in the same cage.

Individual Characteristics

Just like humans, canaries have different personalities. There are those birds that are more courageous and those that are more reserved. You can readily observe this while the birds are feeding: some will eagerly pounce on every new seed, whereas some wait, letting other birds "sample" the food first. This is somewhat similar to their friendship with humans. Some canaries will make contact first and like to sit on the human's hand and even permit some petting. Many canaries like to be stroked along their chest, less so along their back. However, here too are individual differences; you simply have to try it. With birds that are shy and require some time to gain sufficient trust, speak softly and gently, and move slowly. It is important that you not force your canary. That would destroy any trust already established. Generally, however, canaries are relaxed and amiable toward humans. If a bird has never had any negative experiences in its life, curiosity and hunger for tasty treats often win when its owner shows up. If you spoil the birds occasionally with something special like a spray of millet, there will

These colorful little feather balls will become your friends for life if they get loving attention from you every day.

No problem: It is very easy for some canaries to move small toys—especially when there is going to be a reward!

The Voice of **Canaries**

TALKING AND WHISTLING Canaries cannot repeat spoken words like parrots can. Similarly, they cannot whistle a song heard on the radio. Their biggest talent lies in their own singing, which is part of their natural behavior. Male canaries often sing for hours.

UNIQUE SINGING A male canary starts to sing early in the morning, and also sings at different times during the day. The basic structure of the canary song is innate, but some elements can also be borrowed from other males, especially from the bird's father. Beyond that, canaries also include other strange noises in their song repertoire, which continues to develop throughout their entire life.

be no obstacle in the path of friendship. You can try this out by placing some food on your open palm. Soon your pet will happily clamber onto your hand to retrieve the treat.

Ready for the Circus

If you have a lot of time and patience, you can try to teach your canary a few tricks. Children often have a lot of patience for this type of activity. Particularly tame and playful canaries can learn, for example, to roll a plastic lattice ball (available from pet shops) across a table. The ball is then supposed to be pushed back again by you. It is advisable to practice this every day, particularly when the canary shows interest in the ball. It reinforces this type of behavior. Initially, reward the bird when it turns towards the ball or even flies toward it when you have pushed the ball away. After a few days or weeks of practicing, the bird will then roll the ball toward you without coaxing and will then play "table football" with you.

How Your Canary Shows its Affection

If your canary likes you and has close contact with you, the bird will want to spend a lot of time in your presence. When you are doing your housework, it will watch you while you are dusting or washing the dishes. If you can safely lock up other pets, it might even ride around on your shoulder. What is important here is that the bird is not being exposed to any danger, for instance when you are ironing or cooking.

   Note A particular show of affection is when the bird nibbles gently on you, or attempts to preen your hair.

Games and Activities

Canaries cannot grip well with their feet, so they investigate new items with their eyes and beaks. In addition, they like to taste whether something is edible. Therefore, make sure that bird toys are not losing small fragments that could then be swallowed. Crop inflammations, intestinal blockages, or even death by suffocation can be the consequence.

Play Opportunities in the Cage

You should replace the "discovery opportunities" inside the cage or simply change their positions. Apart from toys available from a pet shop, you can be creative and make the toys yourself.

Natural toys You should introduce fresh, natural branches into the cage, as often as possible, ideally together with flower buds and leaves. The birds will be able to keep themselves busy with that for hours. If there is still bark attached to the branches (especially from willow trees), the birds will nibble on that as well. Be sure to use branches that haven't been contaminated, and wash them thoroughly to prevent disease transmission from wild birds.

A fir cone, suspended by a string, can be a magical attraction—it will become a swing, a toy, and food, all in one.

Available from pet shops You will need to find out what commercially available toys your bird likes or ignores, and which ones are being used most often. There are, for instance, small lattice balls made of plastic, that can be filled with fresh herbs. This way, the birds can reach these treats only through the lattice, and it takes hours to eat all of the food.

Swing and rope A swing or a rope inside the cage simulates a branch swinging in the breeze. Canaries will often play on swings for hours, enjoying the movements. Green feed can also be hidden in the loops of the swing or along the rope suspending the swing. This makes toys like that even more intriguing.

Out-of-Cage Time

If you decide to let your canary out of its cage occasionally, your bird will have fun exploring. Limit the bird to one small room. Be sure to remove hazards and restrict other pets. Things that can be moved will be picked up by canaries with their beaks to have a look underneath to see what—if anything—is there. Canaries like to stick their heads into small caves or even hop inside, for instance into drawers. Therefore, it is important that you be present during all free flight sessions, so the birds cannot injure themselves or become trapped or locked inside somewhere. To stimulate the mental capabilities of your canaries, you should offer new toys frequently.

Warm **Shower**

Some canaries love to be sprayed with water. Warm water sprayed from a plant mister (used exclusively for birds) can be a fun and healthy diversion. The birds enjoy such imitation "rainfall" and will spread their wings when under it. Clearly, they love to feel the water running over their entire body. Such a bath is best administered in a plastic tub.

SWINGS A variety of models are available from pet shops, but of course they can also be homemade. To do that, cut a natural branch to the correct length and fasten a strong wire (with a screw through a loop at each end) to the branch. The other end of each wire must be bent in such a way that it can be hooked into the cage roof. Make sure that both wires are of equal length, and that there are no protruding wire ends that could injure the birds.

ROPES Canaries eagerly accept ropes. This is where these birds really display their considerable climbing talent. Sometimes they even hang upside down from ropes. Colorful ropes are particularly fascinating to the birds, but you can also use heavy coconut-fiber ropes, available from gardening centers. Occasionally you can also attach dandelion leaves or chickweed to the ropes. This makes canaries "work" for their food.

CHARPIE During the breeding season, the female becomes preoccupied with leaves, hairs, and pieces of fluff and threads of all kind. The bird shown here carries some nesting material (*charpie*) in its beak.

Adventure: Free Flight

Skillful maneuvers are typical for these little aerial acrobats. They can really romp around and venture on discovery tours.

If you wish to allow your bird periods of free flight, you must make sure you can provide a safe environment. Free flight allows your canary to build muscles, burn off excess energy, and enjoy the mental stimulation of time outside the cage.

Creating a Free Flight Room

Game and discovery possibilities, which you can offer your birds during the free flight session, have been discussed on page 54. A climbing tree, specially set up in the free flight room, will also be very

popular with your pets. To build such a tree, simply insert a thick branch (or several smaller ones) into a Christmas tree stand or into a flower container filled with sand and rocks. Make sure the branch is securely embedded. Underneath the "tree," spread out newspaper, which then facilitates the removal of bird droppings. If you replace the branch or branches frequently, you will notice the birds spending many hours investigating the bark. A flowerpot with grass seeds or organic potting soil will also be very popular with canaries. They love to feed on the seeds and pick through the soil for something edible. It may be advisable to cover furniture with old towels or sheets to prevent droppings from leaving stains.

Caution: Trap

It is advisable to maintain certain rules during free flight sessions:

› Inform everybody in your home that the canaries are on their free flight. This way you avoid accidents. Alternatively, hang a warning sign outside the door.

› Close the curtains during the free flight so that the birds do not crash into windows. Close windows or at least make sure screens are tightly secured, because these little birds can easily escape through a small opening. Cover mirrors as well.

› Flower vases, drinking glasses, toilets, aquariums, or buckets filled with water can become a drowning hazard to free-flying canaries.

› Cleaning agents, medications, cigarettes, and ashtrays do not belong in a bird room. You should also remove all sharp objects.

› Keep all other pets outside.

› During free flight sessions, the canaries can fall into drawers or behind cabinets or furniture, where they can become trapped. Therefore, you must always be present in the room when the birds are flying about freely.

› Please, no heat sources, such as candles, an open fireplace, a turned-on stove, or a hot clothes iron in the bird room.

Travel

If you have only one canary, you might be tempted to take it on vacation with you. This usually isn't a good idea. Your bird will be safer and happier in the hands of a qualified bird-sitter. If you do decide to give it a try, be aware of any travel restrictions, such as quarantines that might exist from state to state. Check your lodging in advance to see if pets are allowed. Bring a supply of canary food and bottled water. If you decide to leave your bird behind, you will need to make arrangements in advance.

› Neighbor, friend, animal-sitter, or boarding facility?

› Leave your cell phone number behind and the telephone number of your local veterinarian.

› Leave a list with the person who looks after your canary, for example how often the bird is to be fed, cage cleaning instructions, and other essential tasks to be performed in your absence.

Back into **the Cage**

WITH CONFIDENCE If your canary is hand tame, simply carry it back to the cage. Hold one hand in front of the bird for protection while walking toward the cage.

WITH PATIENCE Alternatively, you can wait until the bird is hungry and returns to the cage on its own.

BE TRICKY If your canary is a little shy, attach a long string to the cage door. As soon as the bird is inside the cage, pull on the string to close the door.

IN AN EMERGENCY Only in an extreme emergency should you have to darken the room completely. The bird will remain sitting quietly. Then you can temporarily blind it with a flashlight, cautiously pick it up by hand, and return it to the cage.

Breeding Canaries

It is exciting to observe canaries during their partner selection, courtship, laying and hatching the eggs, and subsequent rearing of the young. They are easier to breed than parrots, and make a good "beginner" bird for budding aviculturists.

The Reproduction of Canaries

Courtship and mating The courtship of canaries depends upon the length of daylight, which modifies hormonal production; it starts about March, but can be manipulated indoors under artificial lighting. At that time males start to court the females, who are collecting the nesting material. Nest construction, which is done by females, involves the use of cotton threads, small pieces of paper, sisal string, hay, or grass. Sometimes a nest is completed in half a day. This is followed by mating. The male hops onto the back of the female and holds on with its claws. Usually the male will maintain its position on the back of the female by flapping its wings. During this time both birds hold the opening of their cloacae against each other and the male deposits his sperm, which travels up the hen's reproductive tract and fertilizes the egg cell.

Egg laying and brooding Four to five days after mating, the female commences to lay four to six bluish eggs, which is called a "clutch." Over the following 13 days, the female will brood the eggs. While she sits on the nest, the male will feed her. The female leaves the clutch only briefly to defecate or to take a bath. During this period you should not disturb the female.

1   NEST CONSTRUCTION Here the female has decided to use a nesting basket.

2   BROODING The female will incubate the clutch for about 13 days. If she is disturbed during this period, she may leave the nest: In that case, the eggs could cool off and the developing embryos inside could die.

3   REARING During this period, the parents should be given particularly nutritious, protein-rich food, supplemented by calcium and minerals.

Rearing the young The naked, blind (approximately ¾ inch [2 cm] long) young will hatch in about 13 days. Two to three days later the first feathers are starting to sprout. At an age of 10 to 12 days, the eyes are completely open and most of the body is covered with feather stubbles. The female will take the nestlings under her wings and keep them warm by sitting on them. Initially she feeds the young with a thin mixture of regurgitated and partially digested food. Thereafter, the young are fed by both parents. The young will leave the nest after three weeks. They are now fully fledged, but the feathers appear to be slightly blunted at their tips. At that point, the young will continue to be fed by their parents for another two weeks.

Preparing for independence By watching their father feed, the young learn what is edible. Only after they have started feeding on their own should the young be separated from their parents. You should make this process easier for the bird by offering special rearing food (available at pet stores) (see page 32). Such a rearing diet should be offered to the chicks until after they have finished molting (during the fourth or fifth month) but in steadily decreasing amounts, so that in the end the young eat the same food as their parents. The breeding season ends between July and August; the parents will then go into their molt.

What to Do with the Canary Progeny?

If your friends and relatives do not want the young canaries, you may wish to consider an advertisement in the local newspaper or inquire with pet shops in the area. The sex of individual birds can only be determined reliably when the birds have become sexually mature after 6 to 8 months (see page 13).

Setting Up a **Breeding Cage**

TIPS BY
CANARY EXPERT
Thomas Haupt

BREEDING CAGE If there is a bonded pair in the aviary, you should provide a separate breeding cage. If you have a single pair only, it can—of course—remain there.

NEST SUPPORT Provide one or (better) several nest supports: small baskets made of plastic, metal, or hemp, into which the female can place the nesting material. Such nest supports are ideally located in a quiet corner, so that the birds are not disturbed while nesting.

NESTING MATERIAL Distribute nesting material such as cotton threads, small pieces of paper, and sisal threads, as well as hay and grass, throughout the cage. The female will select the material it wants for building the nest.

FOOD Offer a diverse and calorie-rich diet, including egg food (see page 32). You should also provide calcium, which is needed by the female to produce egg shells. As early as the nesting phase, you should adapt the birds to rearing and insect food. Canaries need some time until they fully accept a new type of food. They will then also feed their young with it later on.

Resources

A great variety of sources are available that can provide you with answers about your canaries, and about keeping canaries as pets in general. In the first instance, you should seek out experienced canary keepers in your area who may well be willing to share their knowledge with you. Failing that, the next best avenue is to contact whoever sold you your bird, a pet shop in your area, or maybe a professional breeder. Beyond that, there is of course the Internet, where major search engines (e.g. Google and others) can provide you with a vast spectrum of information, depending on specific questions asked. In fact, anything you need to know is available on the Internet. One of the basic yet key phrases you may wish to enter in a search engine is *How to keep canaries as pets?*

Clubs and Associations

› American Canary Fanciers Association (ACFA)
www.acfa-canaryclub.com
› International Canary Society (ICS)
www.3.upatsix.com/ics
› Old Variety Canary Association
www.ovcaus.com
› Stafford Canary Club of America
www.staffords-usa.com
› Lou Abbott Roller Canary Club
www.songtypecanaries.com/louabbott

Canaries Online

You should direct specific questions about canaries to your local pet store or to an avian veterinarian. But, you can find practical hints and information about canaries on the Internet.
› The Association of Avian Veterinarians (AAV)
www.aav.org
› BirdChannel.com
www.birdchannel.com
› CanaryAdvisor.com
www.canaryadvisor.com/index.html
› Pet Bird Canary FAQ
www.upatsix.com/faq/canary.htm

Important Notes

› **Sick canary** If disease symptoms appear in your bird, contact your veterinarian as soon as possible.

› **Allergies and asthma** If you have asthma or suffer from a feather allergy you should consult your doctor before purchasing a canary.

› **Cross-contamination** There are only a few canary diseases that can be transmitted to humans. If you have influenza or a cold, inform your doctor that you have had contact with these birds.

First edition for the United States, its territories and dependencies and Canada published in 2010 by Barron's Educational Series, Inc.

Published originally under the title *Kanarienvögel*
© 2008 by Gräfe und Unzer Verlag GmbH, München.

English translation copyright © 2010 by Barron's Educational Series, Inc.
German edition by: Thomas Haupt

English translation by U. Erich Friese

All inquiries should be addressed to:
Barron's Educational Series, Inc.
250 Wireless Boulevard
Hauppauge, NY 11788
www.barronseduc.com

ISBN-13: 978-0-7641-4430-1
ISBN-10: 0-7641-4430-8

Library of Congress Catalog Card No.: 2009910623

PRINTED IN CHINA
9 8 7 6 5 4 3 2 1

The Author

Dr. Thomas Haupt grew up with animals, and he has made his love for them his profession. He has been working as a veterinarian in his own veterinary practice since 1992. Birds make up a particularly large number of his patients. He also keeps various bird species, principally parakeets and parrots. In addition, he operates a wildlife rehabilitation center for injured animals that are subsequently released back into the wild.

The Photographer

Oliver Giel has specialized in nature and animal photography. Together with his partner Eva Scherer, he works on photographic productions for books, periodicals, calendars, and advertising. For further details about his photo studio please refer to *www.tierphotograf.com.*

Photo References

All photographs in this book by Oliver Giel, except: Picturemaxx 14, 41 right; Waldhäusl: 58-1, 58-2. 58-3.

SOS – What to Do?

Canaries can become prey

PROBLEM In spite of all precautions, it sometimes happens that a dog or cat catches a canary. **SOLUTION** Take the bird to a veterinarian immediately. Cats, especially, harbor a bacterium that is deadly to birds. The veterinarian will probably prescribe an antibiotic that you will need to administer to the bird to prevent infection.

Crash into glass windows

PROBLEM It can happen that your bird flies against a window during the free flight session. **SOLUTION** Even when there are no fractures or other injuries, the bird may have sustained a concussion or other internal injuries. Place the bird in a dark box, where it cannot be disturbed. Keep it warm with a heat lamp, and contact a veterinarian immediately.

Unusual respiratory sounds

PROBLEM If your canary emits squeaking respiratory sounds while breathing, it is probably infested with air sac mites. **SOLUTION** The veterinarian will prescribe a medication that is applied underneath the wings, which then enters the skin and gradually kills the mites.

Escaped canary

PROBLEM You have forgotten to close a window and the bird has escaped to the outside of your home during the free flight session. **SOLUTION** When this has happened, it is important to act very quickly. Initially, such a bird is usually disoriented and remains in the immediate vicinity of your home. Go outside and call the bird. Tame birds may eventually fly back to your hand. Place the usual cage (with food) within view of the bird, which will sometimes return to the cage on its own. Place posters around town, and contact local police, pet shops, and veterinarians so that the bird can be returned to you if found.

Crushing and contusion

PROBLEM Your canary happened to sit on an open door that was suddenly closed by a gust of wind. The injuries sustained can involve severe bleeding, or a leg being completely severed. **SOLUTION** Press a handkerchief cautiously to the wound and immediately see a veterinarian. Canaries can get along well on only one leg.